the Companion DISCUSSION GUIDE for the ATF Teen Devo magazine

[Issue 4 • Volume 1]

NEXGEN®
Building the New Generation of Believers

COOK COMMUNICATIONS MINISTRIES
Colorado Springs, Colorado • Paris, Ontario
KINGSWAY COMMUNICATIONS LTD
Eastbourne, England

NexGen® is an imprint of
Cook Communications Ministries, Colorado Springs, CO 80918
Cook Communications, Paris, Ontario
Kingsway Communications, Eastbourne, England

THE COMPANION DISCUSSION GUIDE FOR THE ATF TEEN DEVO MAGAZINE
©2006 by Cook Communications Ministries

All rights reserved. No part of this book may be reproduced without written permission, except for brief quotations in books and critical reviews. For information, write Cook Communications Ministries, 4050 Lee Vance View, Colorado Springs, CO 80918.

NexGen® is a registered trademark of Cook Communications Ministries

First printing, 2006
Printed in the United States of America
1 2 3 4 5 6 7 8 9 10 Printing Year 09 08 07 06 05

Content: Frieda Nossaman
Editor: Doug Mauss
Cover Design: BMB Design
Interior Design: Julie Brangers

Unless otherwise noted, Scripture quotations are taken from the Holy Bible: New International Version® Copyright © 1973, 1978, 1984 by International Bible Society. Used by permission of Zondervan Publishing House. All rights reserved.

INTRODUCTION

Teens have a hard life. You, as their youth leader, know this. Making the grades, succeeding in sports, work, and relationships requires effort and a certain maturity and finesse. High expectations from parents, teachers, coaches—and unrealistic expectations from the media—make for a tricky road to maneuver. For many, just getting through high school with one's self-esteem intact is the ultimate survivor story.

Although all teens need friends, your role as youth leader needs to be much more. The key to working with teens comes down to this: care for them, be a good listener and someone they can trust and learn from. Above all, pray for them by name each week. Allow your teens to share their feelings without interrupting and analyzing their every word. An open heart toward them is the best gift you can give.

This *Companion Discussion Guide* is for use with the *Acquire the Fire Teen Devo* magazine, Issue 4. Take time to familiarize yourself with the magazine before meeting with your group. The magazine's informal approach invites teens to look inside and discover God's wisdom, wonder, and love for them. The sessions in this discussion guide will allow you to help your teens get a handle on their thoughts and feelings and learn from the process of examining them.

Each session is divided into three sections: **Beginning**, **Middle,** and **End**. It doesn't get simpler than that! The **Beginning** may include an optional activity to grab the interest of the group. If you choose not to do it, go ahead with the lesson. It's your choice. Open with prayer asking God to unite your group, making your time together one of trust and concern for one another. After the prayer, move ahead to the discussion questions.

The **Middle** takes you into the heart of *Acquire the Fire*. Some sessions focus on segments in the Guys' section and others in the Girls' section of the devo. Have everyone in the group turn to the page and look at it together. Use the suggested questions to get the ball rolling. The **End** gives everyone a chance to reflect on how the issues you've raised affect each person individually. Close your time together with the prayer provided (or use your own). Be sure to answer any questions your teens might have.

Music is very important to teens. Play it in the background or to open prayer times. Food makes a great icebreaker too. Leading a group of teens takes energy, attention, commitment, and a sense of humor. God applauds your effort with his teenagers, as do we!

Before you start,

here are brief descriptions of the devotions found inside the *Acquire the Fire Devo* magazine. They expand on the five topics for Issue 4: Modern Christianity, pop culture, community, fear, and competition. The devo titles below appear in each section but vary by topic.

- **Devo 1: Need2Know**
  This devo focuses on what the Bible says on the topic, the basic beliefs of Christians.

- **Devo 2: GODfidential**
  This devo expresses the view of a youth pastor or a youth worker.

- **Devo 3: girl-OUTstanding or MAN-datory**
  This devo reflects on what makes a godly woman or man on fire for Christ.

- **Devo 4: UP/IN/OUT**
  This devo contains a Scripture passage that teaches a discipleship principle. UP—how it relates to our relationship with God; IN—how it relates to our relationship with other believers; and OUT—how it relates to our relationship with nonbelievers.

- **Devo 5: Truth and Dare**
  This devo is divided in two: A "Truth" section—a Scripture passage related to the topic and a paragraph that ties the Scripture to today's teens. And a "Dare" section—strongly worded challenge to the teen to take the truth of the Scripture and make a stand for Christ.

- **Devo 6: Faith on Fire**
  How faith is key to dealing with each topic.

- **Devo 7: The Super Natural Power of Prayer**
  Well-worded prayers for teens to use.

- **Generation My**
  Christian girls answer teen questions.

- **Tribal Wisdom**
  Christian guys answer teen questions.

And there you have it! Lesson 1 is straight ahead.

STAND APART

Modern Christianity!

LESSON ONE

Bible Truth:
God wants us to stand apart.

Bible Verse:
"But our citizenship is in heaven. And we eagerly await a Savior from there, the Lord Jesus Christ" (Philippians 3:20).

Stuff: Bibles, butcher paper or whiteboard, markers. Optional: large bag of M & M's or other small colored candies, and two bowls for each student.

5

BEGINNING

As you start your devotional time, ask God to direct your meeting and help you tackle this topic. Invite members of your group to share prayer requests. Pray aloud or call on individuals to pray for specific needs.

If you feel it's right for your group, have four volunteers come up (a mixed group of girls and guys is fine, but it doesn't need to be). Say, **We're going to take a look at all the similarities and differences in this group of volunteers. This is a timed activity so get ready to move.** On your cue, have the rest of the group encircle the four volunteers and call out similarities and differences they see. Choose one person to document the group's findings on a large sheet of butcher paper or a whiteboard. Have this person write in large letters the words *Similar* and *Different* across the top.

An example of similar might be that all are wearing jeans and an example of different might be each person's hair color. (Remind teens that it could be any of them in the limelight. Encourage kindness and sensitivity, in other words, steer away from anything that could hurt any of the volunteers' feelings.) Allow five minutes or less for this activity, depending on your class time. Quickly go over each list before allowing the volunteers to sit down.

Optional Activity

Here's a fun activity on standing apart in today's culture. Place two bowls in front of each teen. In one, pour a helping of M&M's. When you say go, have teens pick out all of the red (or your preferred color) M&M's and put them into the empty bowl—using only their mouths. Give them a time limit, and see who managed to separate the most candy. Allow your teens to eat the candy if they want.

Discuss:

Q. **What were some of the most noticeable differences?**

A. Answers might include: gender, hair color, height, skin color, eye color, jewelry worn, the volunteers' names, long pants or dresses versus shorts and skirts, etc.

Q. **Some less obvious differences?**

A. Answers might include: eyebrow or eyelash color, clothing labels, sock color, facial features, T-shirt logos, curly hair/straight hair, wearing a watch or not, manicured nails or not, wearing sandals or tennis shoes, etc.

Mention that today we'll be looking at how we are different from the culture around us, or at least how we *should* be. Say: **No matter how similar we are, we all have noticeable differences. This is what makes us unique and makes life interesting. Even identical twins are known to have different habits or likes and dislikes. It's confusing enough that we desire both the Christian and the worldly cultures. We all want to fit in but at the same time stand out. That is what today's study is about.**

MIDDLE

Have teens turn to "Need 2 Know" on page 4 of the Girls' section of *Acquire the Fire,* Issue 4. Call on a few teens to read it aloud. Discuss:

Q. Why do we so easily notice people who are different?

A. Teens might say it's kind of a shock to see someone who is badly disfigured from burns or is an amputee. Others might notice when a peer dresses all in black or has multiple tattoos or piercings. Most teens won't bring up race because they won't want to be perceived as prejudiced, so mention that skin color is also a difference that is noticed. Mention that God made each nationality and that it's OK to notice differences as long as we are careful not to treat people differently based on race.

Q. Why do you think our brains alert us when we are perceived as different from those around us?

A. It's only natural to notice when we stand out or when someone else stands out. Our desire to "fit in" isn't all bad. It can help us make friends, be productive in clubs and sports, and feel comfortable. The problem comes when we desire so much to be like everyone else that we lose our distinctive as Christians.

Have a member of the group reread the Philippians 3:18-20 passage aloud.

Q. Paul reminds us of where our citizenship lies, with Jesus in heaven. In what ways can focusing on heaven help when you feel caught up in the world and culture all around you?

A. Heaven is a good reminder that all of the things here on earth aren't going to last. When we die, we won't be able to take a single DVD or CD with us, even if it's our favorite movie or song. If you were to die tomorrow, your outfit purchased recently from the mall would be replaced with some bright garment that you have no part in picking out. Although heaven might seem a strange and remote place now, it will be perfect and all Christians will find happiness and contentment there. Being with Jesus will be better than any moment on earth that we've experienced or will experience.

Q. Should a person's religious beliefs be kept separate from the rest of his or her life? Explain.

A. In a society where the separation of church and state is often overplayed, your teens may be confused about this topic. They may not know that the Constitution protects their rights to express their religious beliefs instead of the other way around. "Therefore, if anyone is in Christ, he is a new creation; the old has gone, the new has come" (2 Cor 5:17). In other words, we should stand out! When the Apostle Paul converted, he did a 100% turnaround. We should too! It's impossible to compartmentalize your religious beliefs if they are truly a part of who you are, so don't try to. It's important that your Christianity affect all aspects of your life—it's not a separate part that no one sees.

Q. Why is it sometimes difficult to remember that our true citizenship is in heaven, not on this earth?

A. Most of us are reminded of our earthly citizenship with every turn—we see flags, hear anthems; money displays our presidents and heritage. Our spiritual citizenship and heritage are equally noticeable but we often fail to see it—a Bible that tells us everything we need to know, churches on every corner, prayers spoken aloud and sermons preached. For some reason it's hard to remember our spiritual heritage and that we're citizens of heaven…probably because we spend too much time focusing on the things of this earth.

END

Have everyone turn to "Truth & Dare" on page 10 in the Guys' section of *Acquire the Fire*. Have one teen read the "Truth" section, another read the "Dare" section, and a third read the stats provided.

Call on a few teens and ask them what they would do each day if they had just one extra hour. Answers will all be different but what will likely be similar is that they would all gladly fill up yet another hour in a day, even if it only meant getting more sleep.

Say, **Time is short, but especially for teens who find themselves so busy with school, extracurricular activities, and close friendships. We can blame society for our hectic schedules and frenzied pace, but if we look inside, we only have ourselves to blame.** The more modern our society gets with "helpers" like television, computers, the Internet, and cell phones, the more stressed out people are. Even though these things are supposed to make life easier, study after study shows that they are actually doing the opposite. It used to be that a vacation was just that, time to get away from it all. Now most people take all the luxuries of home with them on vacation and can always be tracked down by pager, cell phone, email, etc.

Consider the following questions as a group:

Q. Why is it so difficult to carve away even 15 minutes a day for prayer and Bible reading?
A. Every minute counts. You always think you'll have time later on during the day for God and your Bible, but by then you're often too tired to follow through.

Q. What are some ways you can find time each day for God and devotional time?
A. Invite various teens to share their responses and encourage teens who are struggling with their quiet times to consider implementing some of these ideas.

Q. What do you think it means to be "holy and set apart?"

A. Teens might mention living differently, standing out, not joining in on the partying or becoming sexually involved with a boyfriend/girlfriend, not giving in to gossip, helping others in their communities, etc.

God wants us to stand apart. That doesn't mean we have to be geeky or unpopular…quite the opposite. As we live out our faith, people will be attracted to us. You might not get invited to all of the parties now, but when there is a crisis or your peers need a true friend, your phone won't stop ringing.

Have teens take another look at the stats provided. Mention that if 26% are absolutely committed to Christ and 57% are moderately committed, then there are another 17% unaccounted for. Most likely they aren't really committed to Christ at all. Don't be a part of that group. What starts out as a bit of slacking off can eventually erode until you aren't even sure what you believe. Be committed! Stand up for Christ this week by inviting someone to a youth group activity or even just over to your house for a game night with your family. As you learn to stretch your wings you'll find that your faith will continue to grow, with eternal results.

Close in prayer and encourage teens to pray along:

Lord, it's not easy standing apart. Even though we're not ashamed of the gospel, proclaiming it everywhere is not what we're accustomed to doing. Help us to know how to live out our faith and share it in ways that will make others take notice and want to be like us. Help us overcome the fear that often comes with sharing our faith. Make us strong and help us to impact eternity as a result. In Jesus' name, amen.

WORSHIP—GOD-STYLE

Modern Christianity

Bible Truth:
God created worship to bring honor to himself.

Bible Verse:
"Give thanks to the LORD, call on his name; make known among the nations what he has done" (Psalm 105:1).

Stuff:
Bibles, whiteboard, markers. Optional: photocopies of sheet compiled prior to group time.

LESSON TWO

11

BEGINNING

As you begin your devotional time together, pray and ask God to help your group focus on true worship. Invite members of your group to share prayer requests aloud. Spend some time in prayer for these requests.

Say, **Worship is "in." There are praise bands, worship teams, worship leaders, and worship services.** Ask, **What does worship mean to you?** Have teens call out their answers and write them on a whiteboard.

Some answers might include: guitar playing, singing, modern songs, standing up, hymns, clapping, prayer.

Then ask: **What things in nature make you feel like praising God?** Have the group members call out their answers to this question as well and note their answers on the whiteboard.

Some answers might include: a sunrise, a sunset, the ocean, animals, the changing seasons, mountains, beauty, etc.

Optional Activity

Prior to the group time, compile a paper that lists various aspects of worship that occur in your church, for example singing hymns, singing praise songs, group prayer, individual prayer, instrumentals, solos, choir singing, prayer requests, offering, communion, baptism, fellowship, etc. List these things individually in a column, leaving space between each one. Make copies of this paper and hand out one to each person.

Then divide your teens into groups, and have each group design its perfect worship service, incorporating any of these aspects. Encourage them to think outside the box, and that they can add any worship components they think of which are not already on the list. Then regroup and share their various ideas. Use this activity to spark discussion on necessary elements of worship, and how externals are less important than the core meanings and focusing on God.

Finally ask, **Why do you think God needs our worship and praise—after all, we're the sinful humans, right?**

Answers will vary but should include the idea that God requires our worship for his glory as well as for us—so we will take note of who he is. To non-Christians it might seem like God is on some sort of ego-trip, but

Christians who know and love God realize that we can't help but praise and worship him because of how powerful and wonderful he is. Also, God doesn't need praise in the way we do, as a pat on the back, rather he commands it because of who he is, God almighty.

Say, **People and churches worship God differently. What's important is that God *is* worshiped.** If you'd like, use this time to emphasize various aspects of your particular denomination and your church's worship style. Encourage honesty and use responses to help you as you focus on this session about praise and worship.

> God doesn't need praise in the way we do, as a pat on the back, rather he commands it because of who he is, God almighty.

MIDDLE

Have teens turn to "Up/In/Out" on page 12 of the Girls' section of *Acquire the Fire,* Issue 4.

Have one volunteer read the long introduction and have another teen read all three Up/In/Out sections aloud.

Ask:

Q. What is your favorite band right now? (Christian or non-Christian.)

A. Go around the room and ask for everyone's input. Music is such a key part of "teen life" that it will be hard for most teens to narrow this choice down to just one.

Q. What was the most recent concert you went to? Where was it held?

A. Have various teens shout out who they saw and where they went. Since teens are really into concert-going, this question may eat up some of your group time, but that's OK. Let the teens get caught up in the excitement of what it is like to see a favorite band or singer up close and in person.

Q. Do you get as excited to sing hymns or hear your church's praise music team? Why or why not?

A. It's only natural that your group members will not be as hyped up about their church's worship time as they are about seeing a favorite band. Without laying on a guilt-trip mention that it's sad, but true that we often get way more amped about seeing a secular band play than we do about joining in for a praise and worship time at church. Ask your group members to contemplate why this might be so and encourage their input.

Praise God with other believers.

The "Up" section mentions that we are to get involved in worship, not just be spectators. It's easy to sit back at church and be entertained, but that doesn't really impact anyone. God doesn't care whether or not you have a pretty voice or can carry a tune.

The "In" section reminds us of how important it is to meet together and praise God with other believers. You can praise God over an awesome sunset or blazing campfire, but those shouldn't be the *only* times.

The "Out" section encourages us to include the nations in our praise. I guess that means leaving the house, doesn't it? Praise is also an outreach. Many mission trips find people interested in the gospel, but only after they've been entertained by bands, skits, and testimonies. God works in many ways, and praise is an important one.

There isn't room for praise in a heart that's chock-full of dirty laundry.

END

Have your group turn to "Faith on Fire" on p. 9 of the Guys' section of *Acquire the Fire,* Issue 4.

Have two volunteers read the segment aloud for the group.

Say, **The word that comes up a few times in this devotional is "repent."** The act of repentance actually has a great deal to do with worship. There isn't room for praise in a heart that's chock-full of dirty laundry.

Before diving into worship time at church, your personal devotional time, or a family or peer devo time, it's important to reflect on:

What things do you need to get right with God today before moving into next week?

- What is on your heart…
- What went on this past week? What things do you need to get right with God right now before moving into next week?
- Ongoing sin you're dealing with…you know what they are.
- Compromising situations you find yourself in time and time again in dating relationships…lies to your parents that are almost second nature, etc.

Allow a few minutes for private prayer time. Close with the following prayer.

Lord, we worship you. We bow down before you and adore you. We're reminded of what we are...dust in your presence. Please forgive us of our sins. Help us to make repentance a regular thing in our lives. Give us new and creative ways to worship you today and this week. Amen.

PASSING JUDGMENT

Pop Culture

Bible Truth:
God can help us in our decision-making.

Bible Verse:
"Teach me knowledge and good judgment, for I believe in your commands" (Psalm 119:66).

Stuff:
Bibles, small pieces of paper, pens, props that could be used for the skits (wigs, ball caps, hats, sunglasses, fake mustaches or beards)

LESSON THREE

bEGINNING

As you begin your devotional time together, pray and ask God to help your group be open to what God would have them hear today. Invite members of your group to write down a short prayer request on a small piece of paper. Collect the papers and pass a few of them out to those who offer to pray aloud. Save the rest of the papers and redistribute them at the end of the session.

Optional Activity

Hand out a small piece of paper and a pen to each person. Have teens write down their favorite TV show or movie title and then write down an old TV show or movie ('80s or earlier) that they've seen. After they've come up with something, allow time for them to compare the two on paper. Some things they might consider are: the rating (or warnings on the show, if for TV), whether or not it is a comedy or a drama, the characters portrayed (believable or not), similarities and differences between the two shows, etc. Use this activity to get teens analyzing how pervasive pop culture is and that they don't even realize its influence until they compare it to something foreign, like the show from a pop culture that's twenty years old.

If your group is large, split in two and allow teens to decide among themselves what TV show or drama they will act out. If your group is small, have teens call out a few of their favorite TV shows or dramas and come to a consensus on one favorite to portray.

Encourage teens to designate actors and actresses (depending on the show chosen) and work through a scene they feel depicts the "heart" of the show. Allow some time for teens to work through their dialogue and actions and then have them perform. When time is up, regroup and discuss:

Q. What is it about this particular show that appeals to teens?

A. Answers will vary. Use this opportunity to reflect on what teens say about a popular show. You might even want to take notes and refer back to some of these comments later as the session continues.

Q. Do you think these characters are believable? Why or why not? (Tailor this question to best fit the type of show or drama your group[s] chose.)

A. Most likely the teens will say that the characters are believable; that is probably why it is a popular show. If for some reason they say that they think the show's cast is "rigged or faked," have them explain their thinking on this matter.

Q. What were some of your favorite TV shows growing up? Why?

A. Answers will be different depending on the teen, but all will likely have had many favorite shows. After many have had a chance to share, delve into what made some of these shows so endearing and/or long running.

Q. Why do you think we watch TV shows and movies? What can we learn from them?

A. Teens might say that it helps them work through their own issues and problems when they see others going through similar things on the screen. Some might say that it is just a nice break from the real world. Others might be so hooked on certain shows or movie stars that they can't imagine life without them.

Explain that TV, movies, and the media are obvious influences on society—Christians and non-Christians alike. Say, **In this session we're going to look at pop culture and how we as Christians can navigate through it in order to make decisions that honor God and show good judgment on our part.**

MIDDLE

Have teens turn to "Up/In/Out" on page 18 in the Girls' section of *Acquire the Fire,* Issue 4.

Read the introduction to the group and then have three teens divvy up the sections UP, IN, and OUT and read them aloud.

Say: **The UP section talks about making choices that honor God. That means it is important to think about God and his reaction to what you are watching.**

Q. On a scale of 1-10 (with 10 meaning "He'd love it," and 1 meaning "This is trash"), how would your favorite TV show measure up in God's eyes?

A. Make it optional whether or not teens want to divulge the show they are referring to, but go around the room and have teens call out a number. Take note and mention how many 10s there are and how many lower numbers are called out.

Q. If your show got a poor rating in God's eyes…why are you still watching it?

A. This will put teens on the spot, but that isn't such a bad thing. If not many teens share, conclude that we all sometimes try to keep our personal and spiritual lives separate. God, however, doesn't like that. He wants to be involved in every part of our lives.

Say: **The IN section gets into how we should question things and see if they measure up to God's standards.**

Q. What are some questions you could ask prior to, or as you are watching TV shows or movies?

A. Some answers might include: Is this show worth my time? Does it have some value? Would I watch this show or movie if my mom or dad or little brother or sister were in the room? What is this show or movie trying to get me to believe? Could I be hurt spiritually or emotionally by watching this?

Say: **The OUT section brings up an interesting point. Keeping up with pop culture could help you get involved in meaningful discussions with your non-Christian friends.**

Q. What are some shows or movies that have spiritual themes to them that could be good conversation-starters with non-Christians?

A. Teens will have their own ideas but you might want to mention that anything that delves into spirituality or that shows good and evil could be used in talking to an unbeliever about God.

Q. How can you decide if a show or movie will help you in your witness for Christ or do the opposite?

A. God gives us a conscience as well as guidelines in his Word. If there is sexual impurity portrayed or foul language and cursing is rampant, it isn't something you should be watching. (1 Thessalonians 4:3, Colossians 3:8). The Holy Spirit will do his job in prompting you if you allow yourself to be sensitive to the content you're absorbing.

Each generation gets more and more lax about what they think is appropriate TV.

Explain: **The Bible, not your TV guide, is the best guide for what is appropriate, helpful, and good. Don't be afraid to walk out of a movie or to turn off the tube. You can even get your money back at most theatres if you complain that the content was inappropriate or the cursing offended you. Don't underestimate the power of pop culture. It affects your heart whether you believe it or not.**

END

Have teens turn to "Faith on Fire" on page 16 of the GUYS' section of *Acquire the Fire*. Have a few teens take turns reading the copy, then discuss:

Q. Why do you think pop culture and the media's influence are such gray areas today?

A. Each generation gets more and more lax about what they think is appropriate. As a result, what your parents might have thought was *racy* in their day in the theatre is now just considered *crude humor* on TV today. That doesn't mean that God has gotten lax though, does it? What is written in the Bible applied to people then and still applies today. God is the same yesterday, today, and tomorrow, regardless of society or pop culture's ideas.

Q. Can you name one or two super-clean shows on television today?

A. Answes will vary. But be careful, just because a show is usually clean doesn't mean that the producers of it won't push the envelope from time to time. Even *Everybody Loves Raymond* reruns could have content that you wouldn't want your little sister or brother seeing. By having an open mind you'll keep weaker believers from stumbling in their faith and you'll preserve your own moral conscience as well.

Say, **This isn't an easy message to hear.** Shows today glamorize homosexuality, premarital and extra-marital sex, foul language and swearing, crudeness, drug use, and underage drinking. If something is inappropriate, it's usually pretty obvious. Paul didn't let the pop culture of his day influence him; rather he used it to turn people to the one true God. You can do the same, but it means using the remote and turning the TV off when you can't find anything that honors God.

Prior to ending your session, hand out a few more of the prayer requests from the Beginning section. After those requests have been lifted up to God, close your time together with a prayer like this one:

God, pop culture is everywhere. Knowing the latest shows and keeping up with the media hype seem second nature at times. Help us to realize that we do have control over what we allow into our hearts and souls. Help us to honor you in how we deal with the culture around us. Help us to find opportunities in pop culture that could be used as a witness for you. Enable us to turn off the tube when nothing worth watching is on. Most of all help us to live for you each day. In Jesus' name, amen.

A GOD'S-EYE VIEW

Pop Culture

LESSON FOUR

Bible Truth:
God's way is always better.

Bible Verse:
"See to it that no one takes you captive through hollow and deceptive philosophy, which depends on human tradition and the basic principles of this world rather than on Christ" (Colossians 2:8).

Stuff:
Bibles, poster board, bright markers. Optional: popular magazines, scissors.

BEGINNING

As you begin your devotional time together, pray and ask God to help you lead students to understand what his viewpoint on popular culture is. Ask students if they looked differently at TV, movies, and the media this past week as a result of last week's study. Have a short prayer request and prayer time prior to beginning the lesson.

Hold up a blank poster board and mention that after teens are finished sharing, it is going to be full of this week's "tabloid" trivia.

Allow teens to call out recent media events, couple-splits, celeb babies born (or any funny celeb baby names they recall), paparazzi mishaps, sports-star arrests, new celeb couples, show-biz rumors, or anything else that the media seems in a frenzy about of late. (As teens list, write down their answers on the poster board using various bright colored markers.)

Optional Activity

Make popular magazines available to your group—teen specific versions as well as magazines like *People*. Divide your group into smaller segments and have teens use scissors to cut out either pictures of celebs they like or admire or pictures of those celebs they really dislike. Go around and have the groups share aloud about the people they took notice of. Use this to point out how immersed in pop culture we all are, even if we dislike it generally.

Have teens come to a consensus on one or two "stories" that are the hottest right now and circle those with a marker.

Say, **The show always goes on. Sure, real tragedies can sideline the media for a time (such as after 9/11 or the hurricane disasters) but after the proper time has passed, rumors once again fly about celebs and trivial "people-dirt."**

Q. Why do you think tabloid magazines and shows continue to grow in popularity?

A. Most teens will say that curiosity and boredom fuel the fire for those kinds of magazines and shows. The love affair with Hollywood keeps growing regardless of the lies told about celebs and in spite of the privacy that paparazzi continue to steal from famous people.

> We need a reality check to remind us that God's way is always right.

Q. Are you interested in the goings-on of Hollywood and celebs? Why or why not?

A. Have various teens give input. Answers to this question will vary depending on your groups' individual interests.

Say, **We can pretend not to notice the "latest and greatest" people but it's hard not to. You can't even run into a grocery store for a candy bar without reading about 12 headlines while you wait to check out. God doesn't expect us to pretend that the up and coming "people" out there don't exist. What he does want is for us to use his words in the Bible as our guide to help us decide who we'll follow and admire. As much as we might want to be like celebs, it's important to notice who or what they often are following: the Kabbalah, Scientology, Buddhism, mysticism, new age thinking, etc. We need a reality check to remind us that God's way is always right. We might not be celebrities, but we're living like we should, and that's really an important thing!**

MIDDLE

Ask the group to turn to "Need2Know" on page 13 of the Girls' section of Ac*quire the Fire,* Issue 4. Before reading the devo, ask a volunteer to look at the Colossians 2:8 verse. Ask: **What does this verse say about the world?** Allow your group to respond.

Say, **The world is full of deceptive and hollow philosophy.** Sure, you realize that today as you look around the magazine rack and flip channels on TV, but was it really like that in Bible times? Yup. The philosophies haven't really changed that much; they've just been redefined. God is still warning us to be aware that *his* way isn't often the *popular* way.

Ask another volunteer to read the first two paragraphs in the "Need2 Know" devo.

Q. Why is it so easy not to realize that the media around us preaches its own message?

A. It's subtle. The marketing is good. It's tied up in fashion and news and other things to make it seem less "preachy."

Ask a different volunteer to finish reading the rest of the devo. Then discuss:

Q. What are some philosophies that our pop culture tries to sell us?

A. Answers might include: Looks are everything; Money = happiness; Celebrities are more valuable than "regular" people; Having 15 minutes of fame is worth everything; Fashion is so important that it's worth splurging on; Thinking conservatively means you're narrow-minded.

The world is full of deceptive and hollow philosophy.

Explain: **First Samuel 16:7b says, "The LORD does not look at the things man looks at. Man looks at the outward appearance, but the LORD looks at the heart." Why do you think the things of the heart aren't emphasized as much in pop culture as external looks, clothes, and money?** Have teens answer. After they respond, say, It's easier to *look* good than to *be* good. Looking good just takes money; being good requires character. And character is the one thing you can be sure to have. You may not ever be featured on *Lifestyles of the Rich and Famous,* but you can develop a godly lifestyle. Recognize that the media is trying to sell an image which will make money. It's not trying to sell character; there's usually no money in it.

First Samuel 16:7b says, "The LORD does not look at the things man looks at. Man looks at the outward appearance, but the Lord looks at the heart."

END

Have teens turn quickly to "Truth and Dare" on page 18 of the Guys' section of *Acquire the Fire,* Issue 4. Have teens take a look at the statistic in the last paragraph of the Truth section and have a volunteer read that paragraph aloud. Say, **16 Internet hours…13 hours of prime time, 12 hours of DJ babble and music and you aren't affected? Of course you are. You can't help but be. Instead of denying that the influence is there, focus instead on the solution to dealing with the bombardment…Jesus Christ.** Encourage teens to turn to him when they feel overwhelmed by the world around them.

Finally, have everyone turn to "The Super Natural Power of Prayer" on page 22 in the GUYS' section.

End your time together by reading the prayer on page 22. Ask teens to think about the things they've been focused on this past week while they pray. Encourage them to turn over to God the earthly things they've been clinging to. Help them see that they're buying more than just a magazine or tuning in to more than just a show—they're being sold false philosophies and ideas.

27

Dear God,

I know you've put me in the middle of my culture for a reason. Help me to honor you by the way I live. God, teach me your truth so that I can filter out philosophies that are hollow and deceptive.

Help me to know when to go against the culture. At the same time, help me to recognize when I might use it to introduce my friends to you. Above all, I want to know you better and grow in my relationship with you.

I love you, Lord. Amen.

A COMMON OBJECTIVE

Community

LESSON FIVE

Bible Truth:
A true Christian community is God-centered.

Bible Verse:
"If you have any encouragement from being united with Christ, if any comfort from his love, if any fellowship with the Spirit, if any tenderness and compassion, then make my joy complete by being like-minded, having the same love, being one in spirit and purpose" (Philippians 2:1-2).

Stuff: Bibles, masking tape, Optional: chairs.

BEGINNING

As you begin your devotional time together, pray and ask God to guide your group as they reflect on what Christian community is all about. Mention that one important way the body of Christ helps one another is through prayer. Have teens share prayer requests and have one or two in the group pray aloud for the requests that are shared.

Use masking tape to mark off a starting and a finish line on the floor, about 30 ft apart (If you need room you can use a hallway or go outside). Divide your kids into even teams of 6, 7, 8, or 9 people. Be sure that each team has a good mix of tall and short, guys and girls, athletic and not-so-much. Tell each team that it must make it across the finish line as a group, but there can only be a certain number of body parts that ever touch the ground. (6 people=3 points of contact with the ground, 7 people=4 points, 8 people=5 points, 9 people=6 points) As a group, they must figure out a way to cross the floor with this restriction. (For example, it might involve piggy backs, hopping, group balance, etc.) Give the teams time to brainstorm and practice their method, then have them compete for how quickly and easily each team can make it across the finish line.

Optional Activity

Have teens sit in a circle of chairs with one fewer chair than there are people playing. Have the extra person stand in the middle and say something about himself. (Can be biographical info, physical, wardrobe, hobbies, etc.) Anyone on a chair who shares that fact (e.g. I have a younger sister) must immediately get up and move at least two chairs away. The middle person uses this opportunity to snag a chair—last one standing is the new middle person. Repeat until your activity time is over. Use this activity to highlight similarities and differences in your community of teens.

Use the questions below to demonstrate that it is a combination of people's differences and similarities that makes us powerful and interesting.

Q. In what ways are all people similar? Explain.

A. Everyone needs love, acceptance, friends, God, and physical things like food, water, and clothes. They can share similar goals.

Say: **Sometimes we can focus too much on people's differences, so we don't see them as siblings and partners in Christ. Sometimes we stereotype people as being like us, and we can get blindsided when they suddenly do something we don't expect.**

We have to remember to look at others as *individuals*, with both differences and similarities.

Q. Why is it good that all people share some similarities?

A. It helps us empathize with others; it helps us find common ground among people when arguments arise; it makes it hard to think of one person as better than another.

Q. What purpose do people's differences serve? Explain.

A. Life would be boring if everyone was the same. This activity was only accomplished because of people's differences. It needed a combination of sizes and athletic abilities to get everyone across the finish line. It takes many different parts of the body to achieve the same goal.

"Now you are the body of Christ, and each one of you is a part of it" (1 Corinthians 12:27).

Explain: **Jesus chose twelve totally different people for close disciples—fishermen, a doctor, a tax collector, a traitor. These guys and others who followed Jesus made up the very first Christian community. It wouldn't be the last though, praise God! Christian community looks very different today but its core is still the same—people following Jesus who are like-minded in their goals.**

MIDDLE

Ask everyone to turn to "MAN-datory" on page 30 of the Guys' section of *Acquire the Fire,* Issue 4. Have teens read the Philippians 2:1-2 verses aloud together then have a few volunteers read the segment.

Q. Have you ever been a part of something that was bigger than yourself? (A team or camp or theatrical performance) Was the experience unforgettable or regrettable? Explain.

A. Answers will vary. Give teens a chance to really share from their hearts about something they were a part of. You may only be able to listen to one or two accounts, but make comments where appropriate to show how a "community" was experienced through this event or group.

Q. Why do you think we are more likely to feel a sense of community on a sports team or in a drum line than we are in church?

A. Answers will vary. If a church is large, it might be easy for teens to feel like spectators or without a niche. In very small churches there might not seem to be room to grow or a place to experience new things. Allow teens to share their viewpoints.

Q. What do you think it means to be transformed into God's likeness? (2 Corinthians 3:18)

A. It means we aren't changed overnight, but rather we change over time as we learn more about God and the Bible. As we grow within ourselves and alongside other believers a morphing of sorts takes place. We truly can then say that the old has gone and the new has come (See 2 Corinthians 5:17). It takes a lifetime to resemble Christ and that is part of fighting the good fight and finishing the race (2 Timothy 4:7).

The community of Christians is important because it is a foretaste of what heaven will be like, when all nations and peoples will stand before Jesus (Revelation 7:9). The Bible spends so much time on Christian relationships because they really do matter to God. It's hard to witness to non-Christians when members of a church body are fighting. Where there are people there will be disagreements...but it's important to work things out. That is what makes Christian community so special; it's a lasting community that will even share heaven one day.

END

Have the group turn to "girl-OUTstanding" on page 30 of the Girls' section of *Acquire the Fire,* Issue 4. Ask a volunteer to read the devo aloud.

Q. Have you ever had expectations for a community event that fell flat or an experience that totally didn't measure up? Explain.

A. Maybe it was a Sunday school class or youth group they were sure they'd fit right into to...then bam! No go. Or a camp they attended where instead of making friends, they made enemies. Perhaps it was a family situation, a new stepsister who made life miserable, or a stepparent who let them down. Allow teens to share honestly and listen carefully.

Q. Why do you think we have higher standards for Christian communities?

A. Teens might say that they'll join a club or something and not have really high expectations but when it comes to Christian groups or activities within the church there is a sort of expected amount of fulfillment that comes with the experience.

Q. What would be a true measurement of success for a Christian community?

A. Answers will vary but some examples might be: A group of Christians who work things out. Christian brothers and sisters who agree to disagree on non-fundamental issues.

Say, **Being a part of a Christian community is something that stands alone. It demands something of us, and it has the potential to be greater than any other group we'll ever be a part of here on Earth. But if this wonderful Christian community falls short of our expectations, it is up to us to help it become something eternal. We need to truly forgive and love each other. We need to relate as fellow loved children of God and not stereotype others. Everyone needs to be loved individually, for who he or she is. Then we'll have a truly loving place to call home.**

Close your time together with a prayer like this one:

Lord, we want to belong. And when it comes to Christian circles, it seems even more important. I mean, if you can't find your place in a Christian community, then where? Help us to realize that we live in a fallen world among sinful people. Allow us to give those around us in our Christian communities a fresh look. Help us also to reach out to new people and put our cliques and groups aside. Most of all help us to find a secure place where we can grow in you. In Jesus' name, amen.

OUTWARD BOUND

Community

LESSON SIX

Bible Truth: God wants us to put others before ourselves.

Bible Verse: "Each of you should look not only to your own interests, but also to the interests of others" (Philippians 2:4).

Stuff: Bibles, pieces of red and green construction paper, pens. Optional: one or two globes (depending on group size), paper, pens.

BEGINNING

As you begin your devotional time together, pray and ask God to help your group focus on others instead of themselves. For some of your teens this might be a concept they hear about often but rarely act on. Invite members of your group to share prayer requests aloud and take some time to pray. Mention to the group that praying for others is a great first step in turning our focus away from ourselves and onto others.

Say, **It's summer and Christmas is a long way off, but it's never too late to plan ahead.** Hand out pieces of red and green construction paper and pens to everyone in the group. Set aside five minutes and have teens write down everyone on their Christmas list and at least one present they'd like to give each person. Use the questions below to get your teens thinking about others.

Optional Activity

On slips of paper, make up a five-question survey on hobby and interest questions. (e.g. What's your favorite sports team? Book? Where's your dream vacation?) Give your teens a few minutes to individually fill out the slips. Don't let them compare answers with each other, and collect the slips as soon as they're done. Then say, **Today we're going to be quizzed on the answers to this survey. But your grade doesn't depend on knowing your own answers, you have to know other people's answers.** Then draw a slip out of the hat. Read the answer aloud, and ask the group to guess whose answer it was. Discuss. This will get your teens thinking about the needs and interests of others.

Q. Do you enjoy buying gifts for others or receiving gifts from others? Explain.

A. Go around the group and call on individuals to answer this question. Or if you'd prefer, have teens raise their hand depending on their answer and have a few volunteers explain their position. Mention that regardless of whether or not we enjoy shopping for others, it's important to at least be aware of other people's needs and wants.

Q. Do you think today's society is more inwardly or outwardly focused than in other generations? Explain.

A. Answers will vary and there are no right or wrong answers. You may want to give your own viewpoint about what you perceive now compared to when your generation were teens. Although there seems to have been a time when parents were overcompensating with material things to make up for the lack of time spent with their children, things might have flip-flopped now with more parents spending quality time instead of mere money on their children. Your teens might fall somewhere between these two trends.

Mention that looking to others' interests is about more than just being polite. It's what God has called us to do. Direct teens to Philippians 2:4 and have them read it aloud.

MIDDLE

Have teens turn to "Truth and Dare" on page 25 of the GIRLS' section of *Acquire the Fire,* Issue 4. Have a volunteer read the "Truth" section aloud then answer the following questions.

Q. Do you think most teens today are more about themselves or more about God and others? Explain your answer.

A. The viewpoints on this question will vary as much as your group does. Some teens will say flat out that everyone is looking out for themselves, that people are selfish, and that being number one seems to be *everyone's* concern. Others, however, may take the opposite approach defending their generation as more caring than previous generations, mentioning charities and fundraisers that teens participate in, and giving examples of teens who have stepped outside of their own circles to do great things for God and others.

Q. Do you find yourself more focused on yourself or on others? How about God? Does he get the same amount of attention as your friends, family, and pets? Since this question is personal, you may want to provide paper and pens and have teens write down their answers. If your teens want to share aloud, great...but don't call on individuals to answer this one.

Tell teens you aren't trying to load on the guilt. After all, you are as guilty as the next person of being selfish and center-focused. Blaming society is an easy out, but it doesn't really give our actions any credibility. After all, the people in Bible times struggled with selfishness too. Although their society was very different from ours, people are basically the same the world over.

Have a different volunteer read the "Dare" section aloud. Then ask:

Q. **Have you ever given up a personal comfort or something you thought was your "right" in order to be considerate to someone else or just to keep the peace (with mom and dad, perhaps?).**

A. Allow teens to share from experience. If teens seem stuck, ask them to think about the last time they flew on an airplane (where everyone was impatient, pushing, and banging luggage onto people's heads) or the role they ended up playing when they joined their last committee (in other words, volunteering to stack chairs but ending up staying for hours cleaning and vacuuming and picking up popcorn kernels off the carpet).

> Looking to others' interests is about more than just being nice; it is the backbone of Christian living.

Q. **What specific freedoms might you give up or set aside in order to win non-Christians to Christ?**

A. Answers might include: biting your tongue to refrain from arguing a point that you know isn't going to go over with the other person, steering away from sharing your opinion on "heated" subjects that could cause division instead of resolution, forgiving minor infractions instead of losing your cool in order that Christ might get the glory, etc.

Say, **Looking to others' interests is about more than just being nice; it is the backbone of Christian living.** These days families come and go endlessly and most only acknowledge their neighbors as their garage doors are coming down. With this prevalent mentality it's easy to lose sight of how important even small acts of kindness are. Be thinking of a few ways you can *really* show interest in others.

END

Have teens turn to "The Super Natural Power of Prayer" on page 32 of the Guys' section of *Acquire the Fire,* Issue 4 and have them read the first paragraph to themselves. Ask your group if they know the song, "They'll Know We Are Christians By Our Love." If they do, sing a little bit of it.

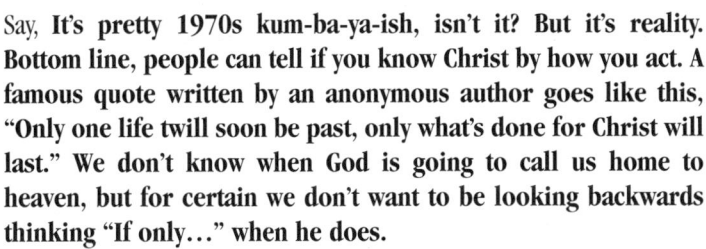

Say, **It's pretty 1970s kum-ba-ya-ish, isn't it? But it's reality. Bottom line, people can tell if you know Christ by how you act.** A famous quote written by an anonymous author goes like this, "Only one life twill soon be past, only what's done for Christ will last." We don't know when God is going to call us home to heaven, but for certain we don't want to be looking backwards thinking "If only…" when he does.

Give teens a few minutes to think of three tangible things they are going to do this week to show an interest in someone else. If time permits have a few volunteers share their ideas aloud.

Read through the prayer and allow your teens to reflect on the words.

Dear God,
I love you. Help me to love you with everything I've got. Lord, help me to love those around me—both those who believe in you and those who don't—so much that it makes a difference in their lives. Help me to

give up what I want for the sake of others. And give me the guts and the grace to forgive, even if the same person hurts me over and over. I want to help create a community that represents you to the world. Amen.

Encourage your teens to follow through this week in making a difference in someone else's life. Remind them that they won't know the difference they can make until they venture out and "just go for it."

Here are some examples of how teens can show interest in others:

- wash someone's car
- tutor a friend
- go to someone's sports game and cheer for him/her
- decorate another teen's locker (nicely!)
- eat lunch together
- volunteer for a local charity/VBS
- help at your church's nursery

FEAR FACTOR

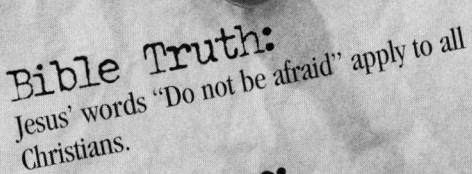

Fear

Bible Truth:
Jesus' words "Do not be afraid" apply to all Christians.

Bible Verse:
"Come near to God and he will come near to you" (James 4:8a).

Stuff:
Bibles, news headlines taped to a large sheet of construction paper.
Optional: paper, pens.

LESSON SEVEN

41

BEGINNING

As you begin your devotional time together, pray and ask God to help your students turn their fears over to him. Invite members of your group to share prayer requests. Break into small groups and pray for some of the needs mentioned.

Prior to group time leaf through some newspaper articles and news magazines and cut out major headlines or gripping stories that could cause fear in people. If you prefer, browse through news Internet sites and print out stories that center around scary issues. Tape the headlines to a large piece of construction paper and pass it around the group during the BEGINNING section. (Some examples might be a flu pandemic, earthquakes, terrorism plots, wars, suicide bombers, hurricanes or weather-related disasters, fires, murders, nuclear warheads, STDs, etc.)

Say, **Some people resolve not to read the paper or watch CNN or click on MSN headlines on the web. Denial might make us feel better for a time but the real fear that bad headlines stir up is still with us. There must be a better way to deal with fear than denial.**

Optional Activity

Have teens form a circle and explain that they're going to write a scary story one sentence at time. (Remind teens that being silly is fine, but gross or inappropriate is not acceptable.) (If your group is large, break into a few small groups to speed up the process.) Give them a starter sentence (e.g. "It was a dark and stormy night, when..." or "Out on the edge of town lived...") Hand one person in the circle a piece of paper and a pen and have him or her write the next sentence then pass the paper to his or her right. Go around the circle with each new person adding a sentence to the story. At the end, read the entire story aloud (omitting anything you feel might be inappropriate). Discuss what made the story scary and why laughing at or addressing our fears can sometimes help us put them into perspective.

Use the following questions to discuss what fears exist today for teens.

Q. **What news events are scary these days?**

A. Invite volunteers to share some of their fears. These answers might range from silly things like spiders to chainsaw murderers or natural disasters. Mention that some people are afraid of things that others are not afraid of. Explain that we need to respect everyone's opinion and listen to the reasoning behind each answer.

Q. **What kinds of things were you afraid of as a kid? Are you still afraid of these things? Is fear something to be ashamed of? Explain.**

A. Some teens might still be afraid of the same things such as fires or storms, most, however will have overcome their childhood fears by now.

Q. **What did you do as a child when you were afraid? Explain.**

A. Encourage as many teens as possible to share their stories.

> "Even though I walk through the valley of the shadow of death, I will fear no evil, for you are with me" (Psalm 23:4).

Q. **What do you do now when you are afraid?**

A. Encourage as many teens as possible to share.

Say, **Everyone is afraid of something. Overcoming fears by coming near to God is the best way to deal with them (James 4:8a). The Bible is full of verses that can comfort you. Psalm 23:4 says, "Even though I walk through the valley of the shadow of death, I will fear no evil, for you are with me." Death is inevitable, but if you know God you can rest assured that he will guide you in your life and lead you home to heaven upon your death. The next time your mind starts going nuts—with worst-case horror scenarios, ask God for help.**

MIDDLE

Have the group turn to "Faith on Fire" on page 36 of the GIRLS' section of *Acquire the Fire*, Issue 4. Ask someone to read the verse at the beginning of the devo, Matthew 24:31. Have one volunteer read the entire devo aloud.

Say, **Wow. Jackie was quite a witness. Some might say she was stupid to stay or careless—putting herself in danger. She, however, seems to have nailed the issue right on the head. When people are afraid; they need God.**

Q. Do you think you would have done what Jackie did if a large hurricane or known danger was coming towards your hometown? Explain.

Christians... replace their fear with faith.

A. Answers will vary. There are no right or wrong answers.

Q. Do you think people are more or less open to the gospel of Christ when catastrophe hits and they are afraid? Explain your answer.

A. Answers will vary. Again, there are no right or wrong answers, just opinions.

As the devo suggests, take a few minutes and have teens pair up. Encourage them to think about what they would do in an emergency situation as far as sharing their faith. If time permits, have a few of the pairs share with the rest of the group what they discussed.

Say, **God has put us on this planet at this very time for a specific purpose. We don't know if the world is going to end on our watch or in another thousand years…but we do know that people from all time periods in history have been afraid—afraid of wars, famine, pain, loss, and death. Christians throughout the centuries have pointed people to God and Christ, replacing their fear with faith. You can too.**

END

Ask everyone to turn to "MAN-datory" on page 41 of the Guys' section of *Acquire the Fire*, Issue 4. Have a couple of volunteers read the devo aloud. Then discuss:

Q. How was Daniel able to face something he was afraid of when everyone else ran?

A. He trusted in the Lord, and he was mature spiritually. The things he was seeing were weird, supernatural, horrifying. But even though he was quaking in his boots, he relied on the Lord to save him if he needed saving. The other men didn't have that level of reliance.

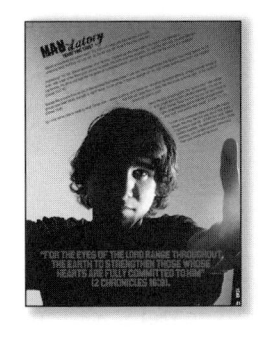

Q. What is the coolest thing about what the angel said to Daniel? How can the angel's words comfort you when you are afraid?

A. Teens may say that it's cool to know that God heard Daniel and was in tune with the going-ons of his life. It's cool that such a being (an angel) exists and can be sent by God to people to comfort them. It's cool that God cared enough about Daniel to let him know he was going to be taken care of.

> "For God did not give us a Spirit of timidity..." (2 Timothy 1:7a).

Q. What fears have gripped you lately? Are you losing sleep over them? Crying about them? Are you online—chatting with strangers—asking for their opinions? Are you worried about your future? Your relationships?

A. You don't need to have teens share out loud, just have them think silently about their answers. If teens want to share, that's OK but be aware that most will want to keep this stuff personal and just mull it over on their own.

Say, "For God did not give us a spirit of timidity, but a spirit of power, of love and of self-discipline (2 Timothy 1:7). Even in the worst of situations God is never further away than prayer. Comforting, isn't it?

Close your time together with a prayer like this one:

Lord, you know everything about us. ALL of our fears. We don't want to be afraid, but we are. Help us to overcome our fears with your help and in turn help others to overcome their fears. Most of all help us to share with people who don't know you and lead them to you so they won't have to fear eternity. In Jesus' name, Amen.

GOD-RAGEOUS

Fear

LESSON EIGHT

Bible Truth: Knowing God is with you can help you be courageous.

Bible Verse: "So do not fear, for I am with you; do not be dismayed, for I am your God. I will strengthen you and help you . . ." (Isaiah 41:10).

Stuff: Bibles. Optional: "heroes" written on slips of paper and placed in a container, large whiteboard, erasable markers.

BEGINNING

As you begin your devotional time together, pray and ask God to help your teens see how God can bring about courage in their lives. Invite members of your group to share prayer requests and pray aloud.

Say, **Heroes. Who are they? Are they the firefighters and police officers who died in rescue attempts on 9/11? Are they athletes in the NFL or NBA or NHL? Are they Hollywood movie stars? Are they grandparents? Parents? Teachers? Are they little kids who dial 911 and save family members who are in danger?**

Optional Activity

Play a game of "hero-nary." Prior to group time come up with some modern-day hero roles—fireman, policeman, paramedic, teacher, mentor, soldier, etc. and write them down on small slips of paper. Have a teen come forward and draw a slip of paper out of a container. Tell the teen not to share who he or she has picked but instead draw picture-clues on a large whiteboard with a marker. (No verbal hints allowed.) Have someone use a timer to keep track of the time (one minute works best). If someone guesses the answer have him or her come forward and choose a different slip of paper. Allow as many teens to participate as possible.

Most of the people I mentioned are heroes, however, how we define hero sometimes makes the term itself confusing. Celebrities and athletes can be heroes, but role model is a better term and sometimes they aren't even that.

Use the questions below to discuss what your teens think about who heroes are.

Q. What do you think makes a person a hero?

A. Answers will vary but may include: being a role model, being brave, risking their lives or reputations, reacting well in a crisis, saving someone's life, being willing to save someone's life even if they didn't actually act on it, etc.

Q. Who are your heroes? People you look up to? Explain how they got hero status on your list.

A. Answers will vary but take time and allow as many teens as possible to share. Some teens may surprise you by listing their parents or grandparents or siblings as their heroes. Have them explain the reasoning behind their answer.

Say, **In the Bible, Hebrews 11 has a running list of heroes.** Have your teens turn to it and have a few volunteers read Hebrews 11:32-40 aloud. Say, **These people endured much more than most modern-day heroes of our time do. Most of these Bible heroes didn't receive any special recognition in their lifetimes, but now have a place forever in history *and* eternity because they are listed on this "who's who" of heroes in the Bible. We'll take a look at one of these unsung heroes later on, Rahab.** (Have a teen read Hebrews 11:31 to see what Rahab did that earned her a place in Hebrews 11's who's who of Bible times.)

Hardly anyone who came into contact with Jesus thought he was a mere man.

MIDDLE

Ask everyone to turn to "Need2Know" on page 33 of the Guys' section of *Acquire the Fire,* Issue 4. Ask a volunteer to read the verse (Isaiah 41:10) and the devo aloud.

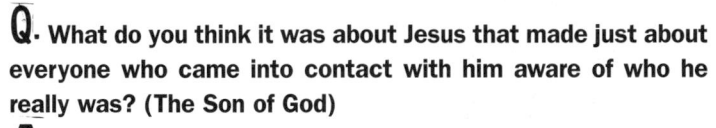

Q. What do you think it was about Jesus that made just about everyone who came into contact with him aware of who he really was? (The Son of God)

A. Hardly anyone who came into contact with Jesus thought he was a mere man. Even if they didn't believe him to be God they thought he was a great prophet, teacher, or healer. The disciples didn't have to be around Jesus long to know he was the Son of God. Even the demons that Jesus cast out knew who he was. Pilate and the soldier didn't see much of Jesus but they saw enough to be convinced that he was not just a regular guy. It was probably a combination of Jesus' miracles and teachings mixed with what most people then knew about a promised Messiah who would be coming that helped them see the light.

Q. So why did the Twelve desert Jesus when he needed them most?

A. They were human. Although they knew who Jesus was and had heard him say he would die and rise again, they let their own fear take over. When their world turned into a crisis, the Twelve were the first to run away.

Q. In regard to their faith, what are the most common fears that Christian teens face today?

A. Witnessing, being made fun of, losing friendships because so called "friends" want to do things contrary to the Bible, doubt and questioning one's faith—What if everything I believe isn't really real? Revelation prophecies, having close non-Christian friends and non-Christian family members, etc.

Sum up: "Do not be afraid." We all know this as Christians. The disciples knew it too, but they were still afraid. When Jesus was with them in the boat they were still fearful of the storm, and after Jesus calmed the storm they became all the more fearful because they couldn't quite believe that they were witnessing the Son of God at work (Luke 8:22-25). I mean, wouldn't that freak you out too? Fear is understandable, but we're called to conquer it anyway. The definition of a brave man is not someone who has no fear; a brave man has fear, but acts anyway, in spite of it. We may be afraid of a lot of things in this world, but if we live for Christ, He promises that we'll win in the end. "For our light and momentary troubles are achieving for us an eternal glory that far outweighs them all" (2 Cor 4:17). In the end, our fears *will* become meaningless in comparison to God's blessing.

> "For our light and momentary troubles are achieving for us an eternal glory that far outweighs them all" (2 Cor 4:17).

END

Have the group turn to "Girl-OUTStanding" on page 37 of the Girls' section of *Acquire the Fire,* Issue 4. Ask a volunteer to read the devo aloud.

Q. Why would God choose to work through Rahab, a prostitute?

A. God can work through whoever he wants. Rahab was living sinfully but she was wise enough to know that the only way she would be saved was to be a part of the winning team. She wasn't afraid to do the right thing and hide the spies, even though it was very risky and being caught would have likely meant her death.

Q. Does it shock you that Jesus was the descendant of a prostitute? Why or why not?

A. Answers will vary. Some teens may have never been aware of Rahab's connection to Jesus. Others may say that it doesn't surprise them because Jesus associated with sinners and prostitutes during his ministry out of concern for them and wanting them to come to God and turn from sin.

Say, **Rahab didn't let her fear get the best of her. We also need to be careful not to let our fear of certain people cause us to shut them out. Everyone needs the Lord—the punked out guy in your biology class who only wears black as well as the introverted librarian who never looks up from the book return bin. It's easy to put labels on people without getting to know them. Often that happens because of fear—we're afraid that we might actually like them or that they'll show interest in Christ…and then what? Invite them to youth group? Are you crazy? Well, what do you think Jesus would have done? Why do you think he hung out with the kinds of people he did? He did it all in the hope that they would follow him.**

51

Close your time together in prayer. If you'd like to, use the prayer below.

Lord, being afraid is a weird thing. We read verses that tell us not to fear and we know our fears are pretty stupid, but we still act in fear time and time again. We know you can take care of us and will meet all our needs (from clothes, to friends, to a great spouse someday) but in the meantime we spend all of our time worrying. Please forgive us for having so little faith in you. Help us to acknowledge our fears and to question them. Most of all help us to be willing to lay them at your feet and to move on to bigger and better things for your kingdom. In Jesus' name, Amen.

THE WINNERS' CIRCLE

Competition

Bible Truth:
Being on God's team is a win/win situation.

Bible Verses:
"What, then, shall we say in response to this? If God is for us, who can be against us?" (Romans 8:31).

Stuff: Bibles. Optional: art supplies.

LESSON NINE

BEGINNING

As you begin your devotional time together, pray and ask God to help you lead students to trust him in all aspects of life. Invite members of your group to share prayer requests and pray aloud for them.

Have teens raise their hand:
- If they are currently involved in a competitive sport.
- If they have ever played on a sports team.
- If they've ever had a great coach.
- If they've ever had a horrible coach.
- If they've ever had to wake up before 6 a.m. to either attend practice or a game.
- If they've ever been a "starter."
- If they've ever been a "benchwarmer."
- If they've ever been cut from a sport's tryout.
- If they've ever been on a Varsity squad or team.
- If they've ever lettered.
- If they've ever received a sports trophy, ribbon, or medal.

Optional Activity

Divide teens into groups and tell them that they are to form a team. They need to come up with a name, logo, mascot, and team flag. Give them art supplies: colorful construction paper, scissors, glue, and markers. Don't tell them what the teams are for, just that it's a competition. When they're done, have them share their team with the group, then say, **Notice how you all were caught up in "team spirit."** Point out how they rallied behind their group cause. Ask them why people get so fanatic about sports teams.

Ask teens to come up with a number between one and ten to describe how important sports are to them. With one being not important and ten being very important. Have teens go around and share their "sports" number.

Explain that we are all affected by sports in one way or another. We might be sports fanatics who live and breathe ESPN; we might play sports ourselves for fun, competition, and exercise; we might never play ourselves but watch a lot of sports on TV; or we might only watch sports once a year on Superbowl Sunday. Regardless of our feelings about sports, it's hard to deny its importance on society and culture as well as its ability to unite or divide people.

Conclude by asking the following question.

Q. How have the teams and groups you belong to been a factor in your life?

A. Answers will vary.

Let's compete against the devil to win people for Christ.

Say, **There is a lot of time, energy, and money spent on sports. Competition is important, but let's take it a step further. Let's compete against the devil to win people for Christ.** Sports are great; they make us feel like we belong. But the main team we belong to is the community of Christians—the church. The sports team we'll take a look at today is one that is huge, has an excellent coaching staff, the Father, Son, and Holy Spirit.

MIDDLE

Ask teens to turn to "UP/IN/OUT" on page 45 of the Girls' section of *Acquire the Fire,* Issue 4. Have the first teen read the verse and the UP section. Then discuss:

Q. How does God the Father work in your life?

A. Answers will vary. Some teens may not think of God as a coach at all. Others might say that he leads them in the overall direction their lives take and is a counselor when it comes to major life decisions. He may also serve as a play guide for what they should do—directing them through life's dos and don'ts through his Word.

Q. How does Jesus relate to you?

A. Answers will vary. More teens will relate to Jesus being a coach in their lives. They may say that they try to live like he did, obey his words, follow his example, learn from his parables and teachings, and feel his love and acceptance in their own lives.

Q. In what areas of your life do you see the Holy Spirit working?

A. Answers will vary. Although many teens might not see the correlation at all between their lives and the Holy Spirit's leading... this area is huge. The Holy Spirit is constantly "coaching" them in their everyday decisions, feelings they have, "intuition" they might feel, stirrings within their hearts, and providing clarity on their decisions.

Have a second volunteer read the IN section aloud. Then discuss:

Q. Have you ever thought of the Trinity as working together to help you live day to day? Why or why not?

A. Answers will vary. Encourage teens not to compartmentalize each member of the Trinity. Rather, have them see how each one has a role to play while working together to further God's kingdom through each person in the room.

Have the third volunteer read the OUT section. Then discuss:

Q. What area of your life is the hardest to take godly counsel in? Why is that?

A. People will answer differently. If possible, share your own testimony and how you've let God into parts of your life that perhaps you used to try to maneuver alone, such as dating, future goals, career choices, etc.

Explain: **God, Jesus, and the Holy Spirit want to accomplish great things in you. By recognizing each one's role, you can better learn to follow their play-by-play instructions. Knowing you're on a winning team and are destined for heaven helps too.**

END

Ask everyone to turn to "Faith on Fire" on page 46 in the Guys' section of *Acquire the Fire,* Issue 4. Have one volunteer read the first two paragraphs then have another volunteer read the last two paragraphs. Discuss:

Q. What interested you the most about this story? Explain.

A. Answers will vary. Many teens will be interested in the fact that these guys weren't afraid to pray consistently after each game. Others might be drawn into the character of the caring little girl. Some may find that this story helps them put their sports careers and games into perspective.

Q. The Bible says, "The Lord …is patient with you, not wanting anyone to perish, but everyone to come to repentance" (2 Peter 3:9). How can this verse give you confidence as you witness to others and make "plays" for God's (not Satan's) side?

A. Knowing that God is already working in people and that he desires for them to know him makes it easier to approach someone and share your faith. How can a person know God unless someone shares their faith with that person? It's a good reminder that ultimately God is building his kingdom and we are just playing parts by sowing seeds, watering them, etc.

God the Father, Jesus, and the Holy Spirit want to accomplish great things in you. By recognizing each one's role, you can better learn to follow their play-by-play instructions.

End your time together by reading the prayer provided in the Girls' section called "The Super Natural Power of Prayer." Read Romans 12:5 aloud, "So in Christ we who are many form one body, and each member belongs to all the others," prior to dismissing your group.

SOUL WARS

Competition

LESSON TEN

Bible Truth: We know what we want; God knows what we need.

Bible Verse: "Dear friends, I urge you, as aliens and strangers in the world, to abstain from sinful desires, which war against your soul" (1 Peter 2:11).

Stuff: Bibles, whiteboard, markers. Optional: props used on reality TV shows.

BEGINNING

As you begin your devotional time together, pray and ask God to help you lead students to understand what their sinful desires might be. Invite members of your group to share prayer requests. Take a few minutes and do "popcorn"—(one sentence) prayers for these requests.

Have teens give a show of hands if they watch "reality TV" type shows. Have teens that do share aloud the name of their faves and why they like them so much. Next have teens give a show of hands if they despise those kinds of shows. Have these teens list the shows that especially drive them crazy and ask them to explain why they do. Ask the rest of the teens why they took a neutral stand, if any did. Ask: **Are there any reality shows that you do watch? What do you like or dislike about the whole reality TV craze?**

Use the questions below to further discuss this subject:

Say, **Whether you like or dislike reality shows, their impact on television can't be debated.**

Q. Why do you think people were (and still are) attracted to these kinds of shows?

A. When they first came out they were very different from the scripted shows and dramas that television was full of. Production studios jumped on the bandwagon and suddenly there were just gobs and gobs of these kinds of shows. Although on a downtrend, the reality TV genre is still interesting because you never know what people are going to do. Teens might also mention that they like to watch kids their own age on TV just chatting it up and being typical teens, even if what they are talking about isn't that interesting to older viewers. Also reality-type game shows have unique twists, unlike *Jeopardy* or *Wheel of Fortune* or *The Price is Right*.

Q. What is most disturbing about reality TV to you? Explain.

A. The stuff can be really personal, like when nannies are in a person's house disciplining their kids or when girls and guys go through each other's rooms and siphon through their stuff (dresser drawers and under the bed included!). The gross aspects of the game shows (eating sick stuff) might also be high on people's lists of "no thanks."

Q. Ask teens to turn to "Is There Value in Reality Television?" on pages 14-17 of the Girls' section of *Acquire the Fire*, Issue 4. Have them take turns reading, then ask: **Do you agree or disagree with Erika's opinion on reality TV? Is there value? Explain.**

A. Answers will vary. Teens might mention participants who weren't afraid to share their faith on a show even if it wasn't always a popular stance. Guys or girls on the *Bachelor*-type shows who wouldn't go along with "mean tactics" but instead were willing to drop out for the good of the person they were pursuing instead of conniving to get him or her to like them.

Say, **For better or worse these shows have shown us people's hearts and desires. Money, prestige, exotic trips, a significant other are all things people want, but what they are willing to do to get these things is sometimes pathetic and sick. Sure, it would be nice to have a large sum of money, but is it worth swindling your own family members or making people believe you're marrying someone who turns out to be just an actor who is already married?**

I mean, c'mon. What has our society come to, right? Well, actually, society has been like this for centuries. In 1 Peter 2:11 Christians a long time ago were warned, "Dear friends, I urge you, as aliens and strangers in the world, to abstain from sinful desires, which war against your soul." These sinful desires aren't new. Neither is God's answer for how to abstain from them.

MIDDLE

Ask teens to turn to "girl outSTANDING" on page 46 of the Girls' section of *Acquire the Fire*, Issue 4. Have a few volunteers read aloud through the devo.

Q. **Have you ever thought of Jesus' life as being like a reality show? What similarities do you see? What differences?**

A. Most teens won't have seen the connection between the two but might see it after reading through the devo. Some similarities might be, Jesus' ability to survive alone in the desert (while being tempted by Satan)—*Survivor* anyone? Jesus' uncanny ability to look at people and know their motives could be likened to Donald Trump's ability to do that with his "grunts" on *The Apprentice*. Teens also might say that Jesus used real words and stories while talking with people, something many religious leaders in his day didn't do—they used lofty words and prayers. Another similarity might be Jesus' ability to heal people and make their worlds better—similar in some ways to shows where homes and lives are transformed (often in as little as a one-hour segment). The biggest difference, of course, is that Jesus is God and the impact he made on the world is unlike anything any human can ever try to duplicate.

Q. **When people in Jesus' time asked each other "Isn't this Mary's son and the brother of James, Joseph, Judas and Simon?" (Mark 6:3a) what were they really implying?**

A. That Jesus wasn't anyone special. That he was just a normal person—not the superstar that people had turned him into.

Q. **Why couldn't people understand the "reality" of Jesus?**

A. They had been with Jesus a great deal (many grew up with him), but they couldn't see past the family he was born into. They had the Savior of the world living among them, but they couldn't get over the fact that he was a man (someone's brother or son) and as a result may have missed out on salvation.

Now, have teens reflect on these questions from the devo's last paragraph:

Q. **Have you spent enough time with Jesus lately to feel his reality in your life?**

A. Teens may or may not want to share this answer with the group. Be sensitive to this fact and use it as a rhetorical question worth contemplating.

Q. **Does spending time in his Word make you feel like you're ready to compete spiritually?**

A. Again, teens might not want to share aloud, however more teens will be inclined to answer this question. Most teens will say that after they have spent time in God's Word they feel refreshed and enabled to witness or to live for Christ, compared to how they felt before reading the Bible.

Say, **God's Word is the key. If you are in it every day, it will be much harder to be consumed with sinful desires.**

END

Ask teens to turn to "MAN-datory" on page 47 of the Guys' section of *Acquire the Fire*, Issue 4.

Have a few teens take turns reading through the devo.

Q. Is seeking popularity a "sinful desire"? Why or why not?

A. Answers will vary. There is no right or wrong answer, however, mention that Jesus was despised (Isaiah 53:3). That isn't exactly popular… but if someone is already a popular person he or she can use that to introduce many people to the Lord, and that's a good thing.

Say, **Sinful desires are lots of things—coveting (wanting what others have), lust or immorality, gossip, slander… We all have sinful desires but we must realize that these things are more than "mere" sins—they WAGE against your soul. That's a big deal. Your soul is your most precious possession. Satan is working overtime for it and there is NO WAY he should even be able to come close to it. But we allow ourselves to daydream about stuff, popularity, you name it. These are those desires, guys.**

Instead of focusing on them, we need to focus on Christ and God's Word. Psalm 119:18 says, "Open my eyes that I may see wonderful things in your law." We need to be praying this prayer each day and have our noses in the Bible, too! If we do this, we'll find that the desires of this world aren't that exciting anymore, certainly not worth our souls anyway.

Close your time by praying aloud.

Lord, help me know how to live in this world of competition, and stay true to your calling: to love others first, and keep from being polluted by the world, amen.

The Word at Work Around the World

A vital part of Cook Communications Ministries is our international outreach, Cook Communications Ministries International (CCMI). Your purchase of this book, and of other books and Christian-growth products from Cook, enables CCMI to provide Bibles and Christian literature to people in more than 150 languages in 65 countries.

Cook Communications Ministries is a not-for-profit, self-supporting organization. Revenues from sales of our books, Bible curricula, and other church and home products not only fund our U.S. ministry, but also fund our CCMI ministry around the world. One hundred percent of donations to CCMI go to our international literature programs.

CCMI reaches out internationally in three ways:

- Our premier International Christian Publishing Institute (ICPI) trains leaders from nationally led publishing houses around the world.

- We provide literature for pastors, evangelists, and Christian workers in their national language.

- We reach people at risk—refugees, AIDS victims, street children, and famine victims—with God's Word.

Word Power, God's Power

Faith Kidz, RiverOak, Honor, Life Journey, Victor, NexGen — every time you purchase a book produced by Cook Communications Ministries, you not only meet a vital personal need in your life or in the life of someone you love, but you're also a part of ministering to José in Colombia, Humberto in Chile, Gousa in India, or Lidiane in Brazil. You help make it possible for a pastor in China, a child in Peru, or a mother in West Africa to enjoy a life-changing book. And because you helped, children and adults around the world are learning God's Word and walking in his ways.

Thank you for your partnership in helping to disciple the world. May God bless you with the power of his Word in your life.

For more information about our international ministries, visit www.ccmi.org.

COOK COMMUNICATIONS MINISTRIES®